Copyright © 2023 by M.J. Knightly (Author)

This book is protected by copyright law and is intended solely for personal use. Reproduction, distribution, or any other form of use requires the written permission of the author. The information presented in this book is for educational and entertainment purposes only, and while every effort has been made to ensure its accuracy and completeness, no guarantees are made. The author is not providing legal, financial, medical, or professional advice, and readers should consult with a licensed professional before implementing any of the techniques discussed in this book. The content in this book has been sourced from various reliable sources, but readers should exercise their own judgment when using this information. The author is not responsible for any losses, direct or indirect, that may occur from the use of this book, including but not limited to errors, omissions, or inaccuracies.

We hope this book has been informative and helpful on your journey to understanding and celebrating older adults. Thank you for your interest and support!

Title: Evolution of Transportation Beyond Cars and Planes

Subtitle: New Technologies and Future Developments

Series: Ride Through Time: The Story of World Vehicles

By M.J. Knightly

"The transportation industry is on the brink of a revolution, with advancements in autonomous vehicles, electric cars, and new modes of transportation like hyperloops and vertical takeoff and landing aircrafts."
Mary Barra, CEO of General Motors

"Innovation in transportation is not only about speed and efficiency, but also about sustainability and reducing our impact on the environment."
Patricia Espinosa, Executive Secretary of the United Nations Framework Convention on Climate Change

"The future of transportation will be about creating a seamless and integrated experience, where different modes of transportation work together to get people where they need to go."
Dara Khosrowshahi, CEO of Uber

"The age of electric vehicles is here, and it's exciting to see how technology is driving the transformation of our transportation systems."
Elon Musk, CEO of Tesla and SpaceX

"Transportation is not just about getting from point A to point B, it's about the freedom and opportunities that come with mobility. Innovations in transportation are critical for empowering individuals and communities around the world."
Ban Ki-moon, former Secretary-General of the United Nations

"As transportation continues to evolve, we have the opportunity to create a more equitable and accessible system that benefits all people, regardless of their background or circumstances."
Keisha Lance Bottoms, former mayor of Atlanta, Georgia

"Innovation is key to unlocking the potential of transportation, and we need to encourage and invest in new ideas and technologies that will shape the future of mobility."
Hiroto Saikawa, former CEO of Nissan Motor Company

Table of Contents

Introduction 8
The need for alternative modes of transportation 8
The impact of transportation on the environment 11
The emergence of new technologies for transportation . 14
Chapter 1: Ships and Boats 17
The current state of shipping and boating 17
The impact of shipping and boating on the environment 20
Alternative fuels and technologies for ships and boats .. 23
Future developments in shipping and boating 26
Chapter 2: Trains and Railways 29
The current state of railways and trains 29
The impact of railways and trains on the environment . 32
Alternative fuels and technologies for trains and railways 34
Future developments in railways and trains 37
Chapter 3: Buses and Public Transit 40
The current state of public transit 40
The impact of buses and public transit on the environment 43
Alternative fuels and technologies for buses and public transit 47
Future developments in buses and public transit 50

Chapter 4: Bikes and Pedestrian Transportation .. 53
The current state of biking and pedestrian transportation 53
The impact of biking and pedestrian transportation on the environment 55
Alternative fuels and technologies for bikes and pedestrian transportation 59
Future developments in biking and pedestrian transportation 62

Chapter 5: Drones and Flying Cars 65
The current state of drones and flying cars 65
The potential of drones and flying cars for transportation 69
The impact of drones and flying cars on the environment 72
Future developments in drones and flying cars 75

Chapter 6: Space Travel and Interplanetary Transportation 78
The current state of space travel and interplanetary transportation 78
The potential of space travel and interplanetary transportation for future transportation needs 82
The impact of space travel and interplanetary transportation on the environment 85

Future developments in space travel and interplanetary transportation 87
Conclusion 91
The importance of developing alternative modes of transportation 91
The potential of new technologies for transportation 94
The need for collaboration between industries and governments for a sustainable future 97
Key Terms and Definitions 100
Supporting Materials 102

Introduction

The need for alternative modes of transportation

The transportation sector has played a significant role in shaping our modern world. It has enabled economic growth, technological advancement, and global connectivity. However, transportation has also had a significant impact on the environment, contributing to pollution, climate change, and other environmental problems. To address these issues, there is a growing need for alternative modes of transportation that are sustainable, efficient, and eco-friendly.

The need for alternative modes of transportation:

The current transportation system, which relies heavily on automobiles and airplanes, has several limitations. One of the most significant limitations is its impact on the environment. Automobiles and airplanes are major contributors to greenhouse gas emissions, which are the primary cause of climate change. They also contribute to air pollution, noise pollution, and other environmental problems.

Another limitation of the current transportation system is its inefficiency. Traffic congestion, long commute times, and limited mobility options can make it difficult for people to access education, employment, and other essential services. This can have a significant impact on the quality of life and economic opportunities for individuals and communities.

To address these challenges, there is a growing need for alternative modes of transportation. Alternative modes of transportation can provide more sustainable, efficient, and eco-friendly options for individuals and communities. They can also improve access to essential services and economic opportunities.

Examples of alternative modes of transportation:

There are many different types of alternative modes of transportation that are emerging or already in use. Some examples include:

1. Electric vehicles: Electric vehicles are becoming increasingly popular as a more eco-friendly alternative to traditional gasoline-powered cars. They produce zero emissions and can be charged using renewable energy sources like solar or wind power.

2. Public transportation: Public transportation, such as buses and trains, can provide more efficient and eco-friendly options for commuting and traveling. They can also improve access to education, employment, and other essential services.

3. Biking and walking: Biking and walking are both eco-friendly and healthy alternatives to driving. They can also provide an enjoyable and low-cost way to explore communities and nature.

4. Hyperloops and high-speed trains: Hyperloops and high-speed trains can provide faster and more efficient transportation options for long-distance travel. They can also reduce the environmental impact of transportation by reducing emissions and energy consumption.

Conclusion:

The need for alternative modes of transportation is becoming increasingly important as we strive to create a more sustainable and equitable world. By exploring and adopting alternative modes of transportation, we can reduce our impact on the environment, improve access to essential services, and create more efficient and enjoyable transportation options for individuals and communities.

The impact of transportation on the environment

Transportation has had a significant impact on the environment, contributing to pollution, climate change, and other environmental problems. In this section, we will explore the different ways in which transportation affects the environment, including air pollution, greenhouse gas emissions, and other environmental impacts.

Air Pollution:

One of the most significant environmental impacts of transportation is air pollution. Automobiles and airplanes are major contributors to air pollution, releasing pollutants like nitrogen oxides, particulate matter, and volatile organic compounds. These pollutants can have harmful effects on human health, causing respiratory problems, cardiovascular disease, and other health issues.

In addition to the direct health impacts, air pollution can also have environmental impacts, contributing to acid rain, ozone depletion, and other environmental problems. It can also have economic impacts, such as reduced agricultural yields, damage to buildings and infrastructure, and increased healthcare costs.

Greenhouse Gas Emissions:

Transportation is also a major contributor to greenhouse gas emissions, which are the primary cause of climate change. Automobiles and airplanes are responsible for a significant portion of these emissions, releasing carbon dioxide, methane, and other greenhouse gases into the atmosphere.

The impacts of climate change, such as rising sea levels, more frequent and severe natural disasters, and changes in ecosystems, can have far-reaching environmental and social impacts. These impacts can be particularly severe for vulnerable communities, such as low-income communities and communities of color.

Other Environmental Impacts:

In addition to air pollution and greenhouse gas emissions, transportation can also have other environmental impacts, such as noise pollution, habitat destruction, and water pollution. These impacts can have harmful effects on ecosystems and wildlife, as well as on human health and well-being.

For example, transportation infrastructure, such as highways and railways, can fragment habitats and disrupt migration patterns for wildlife. Noise pollution from transportation can also have negative impacts on wildlife and human health, contributing to stress, sleep disturbances, and other health issues.

Conclusion:

Transportation has had a significant impact on the environment, contributing to air pollution, greenhouse gas emissions, and other environmental problems. As we explore alternative modes of transportation and work to create more sustainable transportation systems, it is important to consider the environmental impacts of transportation and take steps to mitigate these impacts. By adopting more sustainable and eco-friendly modes of transportation, we can help to reduce our impact on the environment and create a more sustainable future.

The emergence of new technologies for transportation

The transportation industry is constantly evolving, with new technologies emerging that have the potential to transform the way we move people and goods. In this section, we will explore some of the most promising new technologies for transportation, including autonomous vehicles, hyperloops, and vertical takeoff and landing (VTOL) aircraft.

Autonomous Vehicles:

Autonomous vehicles, also known as self-driving cars, have the potential to revolutionize the way we travel. These vehicles use sensors, cameras, and other technology to navigate roads and highways without the need for a human driver. This could lead to safer and more efficient transportation, as well as reduced traffic congestion and improved access to transportation for people who are unable to drive, such as the elderly and disabled.

However, there are also concerns about the safety and reliability of autonomous vehicles, as well as potential impacts on employment and the economy. As these technologies continue to develop, it will be important to carefully consider the potential benefits and drawbacks of autonomous vehicles.

Hyperloops:

Hyperloops are a new form of transportation that use magnetic levitation and vacuum-sealed tubes to transport people and goods at high speeds. This technology has the potential to dramatically reduce travel times and improve connectivity between cities and regions. Hyperloop systems are currently being developed in several countries around the world, and some experts predict that they could be in use within the next decade.

However, there are also concerns about the safety, feasibility, and cost-effectiveness of hyperloop systems. It will be important to carefully evaluate these factors as hyperloop technologies continue to develop.

Vertical Takeoff and Landing (VTOL) Aircraft:

VTOL aircraft are a new form of aircraft that can take off and land vertically, similar to a helicopter. These aircraft have the potential to provide more efficient and flexible transportation options, particularly for urban areas where traditional airports and runways may not be feasible.

Several companies are currently developing VTOL aircraft for use in passenger transportation, cargo delivery, and other applications. However, there are also concerns about the safety, noise, and regulatory challenges associated with these new technologies.

Conclusion:

The emergence of new technologies for transportation, such as autonomous vehicles, hyperloops, and VTOL aircraft, has the potential to transform the way we move people and goods. While these technologies offer many potential benefits, they also raise important questions and concerns about safety, reliability, and environmental impacts. As we continue to explore these new technologies and develop more sustainable and efficient transportation systems, it will be important to carefully evaluate the potential benefits and drawbacks and ensure that we are creating transportation systems that are safe, equitable, and sustainable.

Chapter 1: Ships and Boats
The current state of shipping and boating

Shipping and boating have been a crucial aspect of global transportation for centuries. Today, they remain a critical component of global trade, providing cost-effective and efficient transportation of goods and people across oceans and waterways.

The current state of shipping and boating industry is characterized by a wide range of vessels, from small fishing boats and pleasure crafts to giant cargo ships and tankers. The size, type, and purpose of each vessel depend on various factors, including the cargo or passengers they transport, the distance they travel, and the environmental conditions they face.

In terms of cargo transportation, shipping is the most common mode of transportation for international trade. Large cargo ships can transport thousands of containers and can sail long distances at relatively low costs. The global shipping industry has been growing steadily over the years, with increasing demand for goods from emerging economies and rising international trade. As a result, the industry has become more competitive, with new players entering the market and older ones upgrading their fleets to remain competitive.

The shipping industry has also seen a shift towards more environmentally friendly practices in recent years. This is largely due to increased public pressure and regulatory requirements for reducing greenhouse gas emissions and other pollutants. As a result, many shipping companies have adopted more sustainable practices, such as using cleaner fuels, improving vessel efficiency, and reducing waste and pollution.

In terms of boating, there is a wide range of boats for various purposes, including fishing, leisure, and transportation. Small boats like kayaks, canoes, and fishing boats are popular among recreational boaters, while larger boats and yachts are used for luxury travel and adventure sports. Boats are also used for transportation in areas with limited access to roads and highways, such as islands and coastal regions.

The boating industry has also been impacted by environmental concerns, particularly regarding the use of gasoline and diesel-powered engines, which emit pollutants and contribute to climate change. In response, many boat manufacturers have been developing electric and hybrid engines, which are more environmentally friendly and efficient. There has also been an increased interest in alternative materials, such as sustainable composites and natural fibers, for boat construction.

Overall, the current state of shipping and boating industry is characterized by growth, innovation, and sustainability. While there are still many challenges to be addressed, including environmental concerns and safety regulations, the industry is poised for continued development and transformation in the coming years.

The impact of shipping and boating on the environment

Ships and boats have been a fundamental mode of transportation for centuries, facilitating trade, travel, and commerce across the world's oceans and waterways. However, the environmental impact of shipping and boating is significant, and it is vital to understand the effects of these activities on the environment.

One of the primary environmental concerns associated with shipping and boating is air pollution. Emissions from ships and boats contain pollutants such as nitrogen oxides, sulfur oxides, and particulate matter, which contribute to poor air quality and have detrimental effects on human health. The International Maritime Organization (IMO) has implemented regulations to limit the emissions of these pollutants, but the continued growth in shipping activity means that the overall impact on the environment is still significant.

Another environmental issue associated with shipping and boating is the release of oil and other hazardous substances into the water. Accidental spills or leaks can cause significant harm to marine ecosystems and disrupt the food chain, affecting the livelihoods of those who rely on the sea for their livelihoods. The use of antifouling paints and other toxic chemicals in shipbuilding and maintenance can also cause environmental damage.

Noise pollution is another environmental concern associated with shipping and boating. Marine life is highly sensitive to sound, and the noise generated by ships and boats can cause damage to the hearing and behavior of marine animals such as whales, dolphins, and porpoises. This, in turn, can disrupt the ecosystem and lead to negative impacts on the fish populations that are relied on for food.

Finally, the effects of shipping and boating on the environment are not limited to the immediate area surrounding ports and shipping lanes. The transport of goods by ship and boat often involves the burning of fossil fuels, contributing to global climate change and ocean acidification. This, in turn, can have a range of impacts on the environment, including sea level rise, more frequent and severe weather events, and changes in ocean chemistry that can harm marine ecosystems.

In conclusion, the environmental impact of shipping and boating is significant and multifaceted, encompassing issues such as air pollution, water pollution, noise pollution, and climate change. While efforts have been made to mitigate the environmental impact of these activities, it is clear that more needs to be done to promote sustainable and environmentally friendly shipping and boating practices.

Alternative fuels and technologies for ships and boats

As the negative impact of traditional fuels on the environment becomes more evident, the shipping and boating industries are increasingly looking towards alternative fuels and technologies to power their vessels. This chapter will explore some of the most promising options for ships and boats, including:

1. LNG (Liquified Natural Gas): One alternative fuel for ships is LNG, which has lower emissions of sulfur oxides and particulate matter than traditional heavy fuel oil. In addition, LNG produces fewer greenhouse gas emissions than traditional fuels, making it an attractive option for reducing the carbon footprint of the shipping industry.

2. Hydrogen: Hydrogen fuel cells are becoming more popular for use in shipping, as they produce only water and heat as byproducts. However, the production and transport of hydrogen can still have environmental impacts, and the technology is currently expensive.

3. Biofuels: Biofuels made from plant-based sources such as algae or used cooking oil have the potential to reduce greenhouse gas emissions and improve air quality. However, there are concerns about the sustainability of some types of biofuels and their impact on food security.

4. Wind Power: Sails have been used to power ships for centuries, but modern technology has led to the development of more advanced systems such as wind turbines and kites. These technologies can reduce fuel consumption and greenhouse gas emissions, but their effectiveness depends on factors such as wind conditions and vessel design.

5. Electric and Hybrid Propulsion: Electric and hybrid propulsion systems are becoming more popular for smaller boats and yachts, with some larger vessels also exploring these options. Electric propulsion produces no emissions and has lower fuel costs, but limitations such as range and charging infrastructure remain.

6. Fuel Cells: Fuel cells can use a variety of fuels, including hydrogen and natural gas, to generate electricity. They are highly efficient and produce no emissions, making them an attractive option for reducing the environmental impact of shipping.

7. Solar Power: Solar panels can be used to power auxiliary systems on ships, such as lighting and communication systems. While solar power cannot provide the main propulsion for ships and boats, it can help reduce the overall energy consumption and environmental impact.

In addition to alternative fuels, there are also technologies being developed to improve the efficiency of ships and reduce their impact on the environment. These include:

1. Hull Design: Advances in hull design can reduce drag and improve fuel efficiency, leading to lower emissions and operating costs.

2. Propulsion Efficiency: Improvements in propulsion efficiency, such as the use of more efficient propellers, can also reduce fuel consumption and emissions.

3. Waste Management: Improved waste management systems on ships can reduce the amount of waste generated and minimize its impact on the environment.

4. Ballast Water Treatment: Ballast water can introduce invasive species to new environments, causing ecological damage. Technologies for treating ballast water can help mitigate this problem.

As the technology for alternative fuels and propulsion systems continues to improve, the shipping and boating industries have the potential to significantly reduce their impact on the environment. However, there are still challenges to overcome, including the high cost of some technologies and the need for infrastructure and regulatory support.

Future developments in shipping and boating

The shipping and boating industries are continuously evolving to meet the demands of modern society while also addressing concerns about sustainability and environmental impact. In this chapter, we will explore some of the future developments in shipping and boating, including technological advancements and changes in industry practices.

1. Digitalization

One of the most significant developments in the shipping industry is the increased use of digital technologies. This includes the use of sensors, data analytics, and other technologies to optimize vessel performance and improve safety. For example, digital twin technology can help ship operators simulate vessel performance in real-time, allowing them to identify and address potential problems before they become major issues. The use of data analytics can also help operators optimize vessel routes to reduce fuel consumption and greenhouse gas emissions.

2. Autonomous Shipping

Another emerging technology in the shipping industry is autonomous shipping. This involves the use of unmanned vessels that can operate without a crew on board. While this technology is still in its early stages, it has the potential to revolutionize the industry by reducing labor costs, improving safety, and reducing emissions. Autonomous ships could also operate 24/7, which would increase efficiency and reduce transit times.

3. Alternative Fuels

The shipping industry is also exploring alternative fuels to reduce its environmental impact. One promising fuel source is liquefied natural gas (LNG), which can reduce greenhouse gas emissions by up to 20% compared to traditional fuels. The use of biofuels, such as biodiesel, is also being explored as a potential alternative fuel source for ships.

4. Sustainable Ship Design

In addition to alternative fuels, sustainable ship design is also being explored as a way to reduce the environmental impact of the shipping industry. This includes the use of lightweight materials, improved hull designs, and the incorporation of renewable energy sources such as wind and solar power. One example of sustainable ship design is the use of hybrid vessels that combine traditional fuel sources with renewable energy sources to reduce emissions.

5. E-commerce and Last-Mile Delivery

The rise of e-commerce and online shopping has also had a significant impact on the shipping industry. The increasing demand for fast and reliable delivery has led to the development of new technologies and delivery methods, such as drone delivery and autonomous delivery vehicles. These technologies have the potential to reduce delivery times and improve efficiency, while also reducing the environmental impact of last-mile delivery.

In conclusion, the shipping and boating industries are constantly evolving to meet the demands of a changing world. From digitalization and autonomous shipping to alternative fuels and sustainable ship design, the industry is exploring new technologies and practices to reduce its environmental impact and improve efficiency. These developments are crucial to ensuring a sustainable future for the industry and the planet.

Chapter 2: Trains and Railways

The current state of railways and trains

The current state of railways and trains is marked by significant advances in technology and efficiency, as well as ongoing challenges related to safety, funding, and accessibility. Trains and railways are a vital part of transportation infrastructure worldwide, serving both passengers and cargo.

In terms of passenger travel, railways are often considered an efficient and reliable mode of transportation, particularly for longer distances. High-speed trains, such as Japan's Shinkansen and France's TGV, have become increasingly popular in recent years, offering comfortable and convenient travel options that can compete with air travel on some routes. In addition, commuter trains and urban transit systems provide an essential service for millions of people each day, particularly in densely populated areas where driving can be impractical or time-consuming.

Railways also play a significant role in the transportation of goods and commodities, with freight trains moving vast quantities of cargo across continents. Rail transport is particularly well-suited for heavy and bulky items, such as coal, grain, and construction materials. In some cases, intermodal shipping combines rail transport with other modes, such as trucks and ships, to move goods efficiently and cost-effectively.

Despite these advantages, railways face a number of challenges in the modern era. One significant issue is safety, particularly at railway crossings and in areas where trains share the track with pedestrians or vehicles. Rail accidents can have devastating consequences, and safety improvements are an ongoing priority for the industry.

Another challenge is funding, with many railways struggling to maintain and upgrade aging infrastructure. This is particularly true in regions where railways have been historically underfunded or where there is limited political will to invest in public transportation. In some cases, privatization has led to improvements in efficiency and innovation, but it has also raised concerns about accessibility and affordability.

Looking forward, the future of railways and trains is likely to be shaped by continued advances in technology, such as the use of automation and artificial intelligence to improve safety and efficiency. High-speed rail is likely to become even more prevalent, particularly in regions with large populations and congested transportation networks. At the same time, there is growing interest in alternative fuel sources for trains, such as hydrogen fuel cells and battery-electric systems, which could reduce emissions and dependence on fossil fuels.

Overall, the current state of railways and trains reflects both the challenges and opportunities of modern transportation. While there are significant hurdles to overcome, the continued evolution of technology and innovation offers the potential for a more efficient, sustainable, and accessible future for rail travel.

The impact of railways and trains on the environment

Rail transportation is generally regarded as one of the most environmentally friendly modes of transportation, compared to other heavy modes like road and air. However, like any mode of transportation, there are still some negative impacts on the environment that must be addressed.

One of the most significant environmental impacts of railways and trains is the emissions of greenhouse gases, primarily carbon dioxide. While trains produce fewer emissions than other modes of transportation, such as airplanes or cars, they still contribute to climate change. This is especially true for diesel-powered locomotives, which are still in use in many parts of the world.

Another significant environmental impact of railways and trains is land use. Railways require a lot of land to be constructed and maintained, and they can disrupt wildlife habitats, as well as important ecosystems. Additionally, railway construction can lead to deforestation and soil erosion, which can have a negative impact on local biodiversity.

Rail transportation can also contribute to noise pollution, especially in urban areas. Trains can produce a significant amount of noise, which can be disruptive to local communities. This can lead to negative health impacts, such as stress and sleep disturbance, as well as decreased property values.

Furthermore, railways and trains can also have an impact on water quality. Runoff from railway yards and maintenance facilities can contain pollutants, such as oil and grease, which can contaminate nearby waterways. Additionally, the disposal of wastewater from train toilets can also contribute to water pollution.

Overall, while railways and trains are generally considered to be a relatively environmentally friendly mode of transportation, they still have some negative impacts on the environment. It is important for the industry to address these impacts through measures such as the use of cleaner fuels, improved land use practices, noise reduction measures, and water pollution prevention strategies.

Alternative fuels and technologies for trains and railways

Trains and railways have been an important mode of transportation for more than a century. However, the use of traditional fossil fuels, such as diesel, in trains has led to significant environmental impacts, including greenhouse gas emissions and air pollution. In recent years, there has been a growing interest in alternative fuels and technologies for trains and railways that can help reduce these negative impacts. In this chapter, we will explore some of the most promising alternative fuels and technologies for trains and railways.

Electric Trains Electric trains have been in use for over a century and are already a widely adopted technology. Electric trains are powered by electricity that is supplied through overhead wires or a third rail. They are more energy-efficient than diesel trains and emit fewer pollutants, making them a cleaner and greener option. Furthermore, advancements in battery technology have made it possible to create electric trains that can operate without overhead wires or a third rail, which increases the flexibility of this technology.

Hydrogen Fuel Cell Trains Hydrogen fuel cell trains are a relatively new technology that uses hydrogen as a fuel source to produce electricity to power the train. The process of converting hydrogen into electricity through a fuel cell only produces water vapor as a byproduct, making this technology a zero-emission option. Hydrogen fuel cell trains are currently being tested in several countries, including Germany, Japan, and the United Kingdom.

Biogas Trains Biogas is a renewable fuel that is produced from organic waste, such as food scraps, agricultural waste, and sewage. Biogas can be used as a fuel in trains, either by upgrading it to compressed natural gas (CNG) or liquefied natural gas (LNG) standards or by blending it with diesel. Biogas has the potential to significantly reduce greenhouse gas emissions, as it is produced from waste that would otherwise be landfilled, where it would emit methane, a potent greenhouse gas.

Maglev Trains Maglev trains use magnetic levitation technology to eliminate friction between the train and the tracks, allowing the train to reach very high speeds. Maglev trains are already in use in several countries, including China and Japan. Because maglev trains do not have wheels, they are quieter and smoother than traditional trains, and they also consume less energy. However, the high cost of construction and maintenance of maglev infrastructure has limited their adoption.

Conclusion Trains and railways have been a significant mode of transportation for more than a century, but their traditional reliance on fossil fuels has led to significant environmental impacts. Alternative fuels and technologies, such as electric trains, hydrogen fuel cell trains, biogas trains, and maglev trains, offer a more sustainable future for the rail industry. As these technologies continue to evolve and become more cost-effective, it is likely that we will see an increasing shift towards cleaner and greener rail transportation.

Future developments in railways and trains

The railway industry has seen a lot of technological advancements in recent years, with new innovations and concepts being tested for improving the speed, efficiency, and safety of rail transportation. Here are some of the key developments to look out for in the future:

1. Maglev Trains: Maglev or magnetic levitation trains use magnetic fields to levitate and propel the train, eliminating the need for wheels, axles, and traditional propulsion systems. This allows the train to reach much higher speeds and reduces friction, resulting in a smoother and quieter ride. Currently, the fastest maglev train in the world is the Shanghai Maglev Train, which can reach speeds of up to 430 km/h. However, researchers and engineers are working on developing even faster maglev trains that could potentially reach speeds of over 600 km/h.

2. Hyperloop: The Hyperloop is a proposed mode of transportation that involves a system of tubes or tunnels through which pods carrying passengers or cargo can travel at high speeds using a combination of magnetic levitation and air pressure. The concept was first proposed by Elon Musk in 2013 and has since gained a lot of attention from researchers, investors, and governments around the world. Some companies are already working on developing

functional hyperloop systems, with the aim of reducing travel time between cities by up to 80%.

3. Hydrogen-powered Trains: Hydrogen-powered trains use fuel cells to generate electricity, which is then used to power the train. The only byproduct of this process is water vapor, making hydrogen-powered trains a clean and sustainable alternative to traditional diesel-powered trains. Several countries, including Germany, Japan, and the UK, have already started testing hydrogen-powered trains, with plans to phase out diesel trains in the coming years.

4. Autonomous Trains: Autonomous trains, or driverless trains, use sensors and advanced algorithms to control speed, braking, and acceleration, eliminating the need for a human driver. This technology has already been implemented in some metro and subway systems around the world, with the aim of reducing the risk of human error and improving efficiency.

5. Smart Trains: Smart trains use advanced sensors, data analytics, and artificial intelligence to optimize operations and improve passenger experience. For example, sensors can detect passenger flow and adjust the number of carriages or frequency of trains accordingly, while data analytics can help predict and prevent breakdowns and delays.

6. Hyperloop Trains: Hyperloop trains, a concept proposed by Elon Musk, would use an airless tube to transport passengers at extremely high speeds between cities. The pods would be propelled through the tube by air pressure, and could potentially reach speeds of up to 700 miles per hour. Several companies are currently developing hyperloop systems, with some aiming to have commercial systems up and running in the next decade.

Overall, the future of rail transportation looks bright, with new technologies and innovations promising to make trains faster, more efficient, and more environmentally friendly than ever before. While these developments will undoubtedly take time and resources to implement, they have the potential to revolutionize the way we think about rail transportation and help create a more sustainable and connected world.

Chapter 3: Buses and Public Transit
The current state of public transit

Public transit systems are an essential part of modern transportation networks, providing affordable and convenient transportation options to millions of people every day. The term "public transit" refers to various modes of transportation that are accessible to the general public and operated by government agencies or private companies. These modes include buses, subways, light rail systems, and commuter trains, among others.

In recent years, public transit has become an increasingly important topic in urban planning and sustainable development. As cities continue to grow and traffic congestion worsens, the need for efficient and reliable public transit systems has become more pressing than ever before.

The current state of public transit varies widely around the world. In many developed countries, such as Japan, France, and Germany, public transit systems are well-established and heavily utilized, with extensive networks of trains, subways, and buses serving both urban and rural areas. In other countries, such as the United States, public transit is less widespread and often underfunded, leading to overcrowding, delays, and limited service in many areas.

One of the most significant challenges facing public transit systems is ensuring that they are accessible and convenient for all users, regardless of their socioeconomic status or physical abilities. Many cities have implemented various measures to address these issues, such as offering discounted fares for low-income riders, providing wheelchair accessibility on buses and trains, and installing bike racks and other amenities to encourage multimodal transportation.

In addition to providing affordable and accessible transportation options, public transit systems can also have significant environmental benefits. By reducing the number of cars on the road, public transit can help to lower emissions and improve air quality in urban areas. Some cities have also begun to explore the use of alternative fuels, such as electric or hydrogen-powered buses and trains, to further reduce the environmental impact of public transit.

Despite these benefits, public transit systems face many challenges in the coming years. As cities continue to grow and become more densely populated, it will be increasingly important to invest in efficient and sustainable public transit infrastructure. Additionally, new technologies such as autonomous vehicles and ride-sharing services are rapidly changing the transportation landscape, presenting both opportunities and challenges for public transit systems.

Overall, the current state of public transit around the world is a mixed picture, with some regions benefiting from robust and reliable transportation networks, while others struggle with limited resources and outdated infrastructure. Nonetheless, as the need for sustainable and accessible transportation options continues to grow, public transit will undoubtedly play an increasingly important role in shaping the future of transportation.

The impact of buses and public transit on the environment

Buses and public transit have long been a reliable mode of transportation for millions of people worldwide. From traditional buses to modern rapid transit systems, they provide affordable and accessible transportation to communities of all sizes. However, as with any mode of transportation, they have their impact on the environment. In this section, we will examine the impact of buses and public transit on the environment.

Impact of Buses and Public Transit on the Environment:

1. Greenhouse Gas Emissions:

Buses and public transit systems contribute significantly to greenhouse gas emissions, which are a major contributor to climate change. These emissions come primarily from the combustion of fossil fuels such as diesel and gasoline, which are used to power the buses and trains. In addition to carbon dioxide, other harmful pollutants such as nitrogen oxides, particulate matter, and sulfur dioxide are also released during the combustion process.

2. Energy Consumption:

Buses and public transit systems consume a significant amount of energy, mainly in the form of electricity, which is required to power the trains and buses. This energy consumption contributes to the demand for fossil fuels and other non-renewable resources, which have a negative impact on the environment.

3. Land Use:

The construction of public transit systems, such as subway lines and light rail systems, requires a significant amount of land. This can lead to the destruction of natural habitats, deforestation, and other environmental damage.

4. Noise Pollution:

Public transit systems can also be a significant source of noise pollution, particularly for communities living near transit stations and busy bus stops. Noise pollution can have negative health effects on individuals, including stress, hearing damage, and sleep disturbances.

5. Waste Management:

Buses and public transit systems also generate a significant amount of waste, including discarded tickets, food packaging, and other items left behind by passengers. Proper waste management is necessary to prevent littering and pollution.

Alternative Fuels and Technologies for Buses and Public Transit:

1. Electric Buses:

Electric buses are becoming increasingly popular as a clean alternative to traditional diesel and gasoline-powered buses. They produce zero emissions and are much quieter than traditional buses. As battery technology improves, the range of electric buses is increasing, making them a more practical option for longer routes.

2. Hybrid Buses:

Hybrid buses use a combination of electric and combustion engines, which reduces emissions and improves fuel efficiency. They are a practical option for transit agencies looking to reduce their carbon footprint without investing in entirely electric fleets.

3. Hydrogen Fuel Cell Buses:

Hydrogen fuel cell buses produce zero emissions and are much quieter than traditional buses. They convert hydrogen into electricity to power the bus, with the only byproduct being water vapor. While the technology is still relatively new, it has the potential to be a viable option for public transit systems.

Future Developments in Buses and Public Transit:

1. Autonomous Buses:

Autonomous buses are already being tested in some cities around the world, and they have the potential to revolutionize public transit. They could increase efficiency and reduce labor costs, but they also raise questions about safety and liability.

2. Hyperloop:

Hyperloop is a new form of high-speed transportation that uses vacuum-sealed tubes to transport passengers and goods at speeds of up to 700 miles per hour. While it is still in the testing phase, it has the potential to be a game-changer for long-distance travel.

Conclusion:

Buses and public transit systems are an essential part of modern transportation infrastructure. However, they also have a significant impact on the environment. Through the use of alternative fuels and technologies, and future developments, it is possible to reduce this impact and make public transit a more sustainable and environmentally friendly option.

Alternative fuels and technologies for buses and public transit

The transportation industry is rapidly evolving, and the need to reduce greenhouse gas emissions has become a top priority. Buses and public transit systems are an essential component of the transportation sector, and there is a growing demand for more sustainable and efficient transit options. One way to achieve this is through the use of alternative fuels and technologies. In this chapter, we will explore the various alternative fuels and technologies that are being used or tested in buses and public transit systems.

Electric Buses

Electric buses have been gaining popularity as an alternative to diesel-powered buses. These buses are powered by electricity, which is stored in batteries. Electric buses are cleaner, quieter, and more energy-efficient than diesel-powered buses. Additionally, they produce no tailpipe emissions, reducing the overall environmental impact of public transit.

Hybrid Buses

Hybrid buses combine a traditional diesel or gasoline engine with an electric motor and battery system. These buses switch between the two power sources, using the electric motor at lower speeds and the combustion engine at higher speeds. Hybrid buses can be up to 30% more fuel-efficient than traditional diesel buses, reducing emissions and saving money on fuel costs.

Compressed Natural Gas (CNG) Buses

Compressed natural gas (CNG) is a clean-burning fuel that produces fewer emissions than traditional diesel or gasoline. CNG buses have been used for public transit for several years and have been shown to reduce emissions and lower fuel costs. CNG buses use tanks to store compressed natural gas, which is then burned in the engine to produce power.

Biodiesel Buses

Biodiesel is a renewable fuel made from vegetable oil or animal fat. Biodiesel is cleaner-burning than traditional diesel, reducing emissions of particulate matter, carbon monoxide, and other pollutants. Biodiesel buses can use either pure biodiesel or blends of biodiesel and traditional diesel fuel.

Fuel Cell Buses

Fuel cell buses are an emerging technology that uses hydrogen fuel cells to power electric motors. These buses produce no harmful emissions and have the potential to be very energy-efficient. However, fuel cell buses are still in the testing phase, and the infrastructure to produce and distribute hydrogen fuel is not yet widespread.

Bus Rapid Transit (BRT)

Bus rapid transit (BRT) is a high-capacity, high-frequency bus system that is designed to operate like a rapid transit system, such as a subway or light rail. BRT systems use dedicated bus lanes, stations, and other features to improve efficiency and reduce travel time. BRT can be powered by any of the above-mentioned alternative fuels or technologies, making it a versatile option for sustainable public transit.

Conclusion

Alternative fuels and technologies for buses and public transit are vital in reducing the environmental impact of public transportation. Electric, hybrid, CNG, biodiesel, fuel cell, and BRT systems are all promising solutions for creating more sustainable and efficient public transit systems. As the demand for more sustainable transportation options grows, it is essential that transit agencies and governments continue to invest in and adopt these alternative fuels and technologies.

Future developments in buses and public transit

Public transit is a vital component of urban transportation infrastructure, and as cities grow and populations increase, the demand for more efficient and sustainable transit options continues to rise. Advances in technology and changing social and environmental priorities have led to a range of exciting new developments in the world of public transit. In this chapter, we will explore the future of buses and public transit, including emerging technologies, design innovations, and policy changes that will shape the industry in the coming decades.

One of the most promising developments in the world of public transit is the increasing use of electric and hybrid buses. These vehicles produce zero emissions, which makes them an ideal solution for reducing air pollution and combating climate change. Electric buses are also quieter than traditional diesel-powered buses, which can reduce noise pollution in urban areas. In addition to electrification, there are also efforts underway to incorporate other sustainable technologies into buses, such as solar panels and regenerative braking systems.

Another area of innovation in the public transit sector is the use of autonomous vehicles. Self-driving buses have the potential to improve safety, reduce congestion, and increase efficiency. They also have the ability to operate 24/7, which could help extend public transit service in areas where it is currently limited. However, there are still significant challenges to overcome before autonomous buses become a common sight on city streets. These challenges include technical issues related to safety and reliability, as well as legal and regulatory barriers.

In addition to technological advancements, there are also many exciting design innovations being developed in the world of public transit. One example is the concept of the "mobility hub," which refers to a centralized location where multiple modes of transportation intersect. Mobility hubs can include bus and train stations, bike-sharing facilities, and car-sharing services, among others. By integrating different modes of transportation in one place, mobility hubs make it easier for people to switch between different modes of transit and create more efficient and sustainable transportation networks.

Finally, there are also significant policy changes that are shaping the future of public transit. In many cities, there is growing support for investments in public transit infrastructure and services, including dedicated bus lanes, bike lanes, and pedestrian walkways. Many cities are also exploring new ways to fund public transit, such as congestion pricing, which charges drivers a fee for entering high-traffic areas. These policy changes are crucial for promoting sustainable transportation options and reducing reliance on single-occupancy vehicles.

In conclusion, the future of public transit is bright, with exciting developments in technology, design, and policy all contributing to more sustainable and efficient transportation networks. From electric and autonomous buses to mobility hubs and new funding models, there are many innovations underway that will shape the public transit landscape in the coming decades. By continuing to invest in sustainable transportation options and supporting policy changes that prioritize public transit, we can create a more equitable and sustainable future for our cities and communities.

Chapter 4: Bikes and Pedestrian Transportation

The current state of biking and pedestrian transportation

Biking and pedestrian transportation are two of the most sustainable and healthy ways to get around in cities. Biking is an especially popular form of transportation in many cities worldwide. However, despite their many benefits, biking and pedestrian transportation still face many challenges in modern cities.

One of the main challenges for biking and pedestrian transportation is the lack of infrastructure. Many cities do not have dedicated bike lanes or pedestrian walkways, and this can make it difficult for people to safely and comfortably use these forms of transportation. This lack of infrastructure is often due to a lack of political will or funding. However, in recent years, more cities have recognized the importance of biking and pedestrian transportation and have started to invest in infrastructure to support these modes of transportation.

Another challenge facing biking and pedestrian transportation is safety. In many cities, biking and pedestrian accidents are common, and this can discourage people from using these forms of transportation. To improve safety, cities are implementing measures such as traffic calming, speed limits, and bike share programs to encourage safer and more responsible use of bikes and pedestrian transportation.

Despite these challenges, biking and pedestrian transportation continue to grow in popularity in many cities. Biking is often seen as a faster and more efficient way to get around congested cities, and walking is an excellent way to enjoy the outdoors and get some exercise. In addition, both biking and pedestrian transportation are eco-friendly and have a minimal impact on the environment.

Cities that have invested in biking and pedestrian infrastructure have seen many benefits. For example, these cities often experience reduced congestion on their roads, improved air quality, and a boost in local economies as people spend more time walking and biking in their communities.

Overall, biking and pedestrian transportation offer many benefits, but they also face many challenges. To ensure their continued growth and success, cities must invest in infrastructure, improve safety measures, and promote these forms of transportation as viable options for getting around in modern cities.

The impact of biking and pedestrian transportation on the environment

Biking and pedestrian transportation have been around for centuries and are often considered the most sustainable forms of transportation. However, the impact of these modes of transportation on the environment is often overlooked. This chapter will explore the impact of biking and pedestrian transportation on the environment and the measures taken to mitigate their negative effects.

Current state of biking and pedestrian transportation

Biking and pedestrian transportation have gained popularity in recent years, especially in urban areas. Many cities have implemented bike-sharing systems and pedestrian-friendly infrastructure to encourage their citizens to use these modes of transportation. However, the number of people who use these modes of transportation is still relatively low compared to other modes such as cars or public transit.

One of the biggest challenges in promoting biking and pedestrian transportation is the lack of infrastructure. Many cities lack proper bike lanes and pedestrian crossings, which makes it unsafe for people to use these modes of transportation. Additionally, the lack of safe storage facilities for bikes also discourages people from using them.

Impact of biking and pedestrian transportation on the environment

Biking and pedestrian transportation are often considered the most environmentally friendly modes of transportation as they do not produce any emissions. However, the production and disposal of bicycles and their parts have a significant impact on the environment. The manufacturing process of bicycles requires energy, water, and raw materials, which contribute to greenhouse gas emissions and water pollution. The disposal of bicycles also contributes to the growing problem of electronic waste.

Pedestrian transportation, on the other hand, has minimal impact on the environment as it does not require any energy or raw materials to produce. However, the lack of proper infrastructure for pedestrians can have a negative impact on the environment. Pedestrians often have to walk on the road, which contributes to air pollution from vehicular traffic.

Alternative fuels and technologies for biking and pedestrian transportation

There are several alternative fuels and technologies that can be used to make biking and pedestrian transportation even more sustainable. Electric bicycles, for example, are becoming increasingly popular as they offer an eco-friendly alternative to traditional bicycles. These bikes are powered by rechargeable batteries and have zero emissions.

Another technology that is gaining popularity is the use of smart bike locks that can be opened with a mobile app. These locks are designed to prevent bike theft, which is a major problem in many cities. By preventing bike theft, these locks encourage people to use bikes more often.

Future developments in biking and pedestrian transportation

In the future, biking and pedestrian transportation will become even more important as cities work to reduce their carbon footprint. The use of technology, such as smart bike locks and bike-sharing systems, will become more widespread, making it easier for people to use these modes of transportation. Cities will also invest more in bike lanes and pedestrian crossings to make it safer for people to use these modes of transportation.

Conclusion

Biking and pedestrian transportation have a minimal impact on the environment compared to other modes of transportation. However, the manufacturing process of bicycles and the lack of proper infrastructure for pedestrians can have a negative impact on the environment. Alternative fuels and technologies, such as electric bicycles and smart bike locks, can make these modes of transportation even more sustainable. In the future, cities will invest more in biking and pedestrian infrastructure, making it easier and safer for people to use these modes of transportation.

Alternative fuels and technologies for bikes and pedestrian transportation

As the world becomes more environmentally conscious, alternative fuels and technologies for bikes and pedestrian transportation are gaining popularity. These innovations not only reduce the environmental impact but also improve the efficiency and safety of these modes of transportation. Here are some of the most promising alternative fuels and technologies for bikes and pedestrian transportation:

1. Electric Bikes:

Electric bikes or e-bikes are becoming increasingly popular as an alternative to traditional bikes. E-bikes have a battery-powered motor that provides assistance to the rider when pedaling, making it easier to ride uphill or for longer distances. They also produce zero emissions, making them a sustainable transportation option.

2. Hydrogen fuel cell bikes:

Hydrogen fuel cell bikes are another sustainable alternative to traditional bikes. These bikes use a fuel cell that combines hydrogen and oxygen to produce electricity, which powers an electric motor. The only byproduct of this process is water vapor, making hydrogen fuel cell bikes emissions-free.

3. Solar-powered bikes:

Solar-powered bikes use solar panels to generate electricity, which powers an electric motor. These bikes have a small battery that stores energy for when the sun is not shining. They are an eco-friendly and sustainable option for short-distance commuting.

4. Pedestrian and bike-friendly infrastructure:

Pedestrian and bike-friendly infrastructure, such as dedicated bike lanes and pedestrian walkways, are essential for encouraging the use of bikes and pedestrian transportation. These infrastructures improve safety, reduce congestion, and promote a more sustainable way of transportation.

5. Smart biking and pedestrian technology:

Smart biking and pedestrian technology can improve safety and efficiency by providing real-time information on traffic patterns, weather, and road conditions. This technology can also provide route recommendations to avoid traffic and save time.

6. Lightweight materials:

Advancements in materials science have led to the development of lightweight materials for bikes and pedestrian transportation, such as carbon fiber and aluminum. These materials reduce the weight of the bike, making it easier to pedal and maneuver. This reduces the amount of energy required to operate the bike, making it a more efficient mode of transportation.

7. Bike-sharing programs:

Bike-sharing programs provide an affordable and sustainable transportation option for short-distance trips. These programs allow users to rent bikes for a short period and return them to designated bike stations. This reduces the need for personal car usage, reduces traffic congestion, and promotes a more sustainable way of transportation.

Conclusion:

Alternative fuels and technologies for bikes and pedestrian transportation are an essential component of sustainable transportation. These innovations not only reduce the environmental impact but also improve the efficiency and safety of these modes of transportation. As technology continues to evolve, we can expect to see more advancements in this field, making bikes and pedestrian transportation an even more viable option for short-distance commuting.

Future developments in biking and pedestrian transportation

The future of biking and pedestrian transportation is full of exciting possibilities. With a growing interest in sustainable and healthy lifestyles, as well as advances in technology, the future looks bright for these modes of transportation. In this section, we will explore some of the developments that we can expect in the coming years.

1. E-bikes

One of the most significant developments in biking technology is the rise of electric bikes or e-bikes. These bikes feature a small electric motor that assists the rider as they pedal, providing an extra boost of power to help them reach higher speeds or tackle steep hills. E-bikes are becoming increasingly popular in cities around the world, as they offer a faster, more efficient, and eco-friendly alternative to traditional gas-powered vehicles. With further advancements in battery technology and motor efficiency, we can expect e-bikes to become even more widespread in the coming years.

2. Smart Bikes

Another exciting development in biking technology is the rise of "smart" bikes. These bikes are equipped with sensors, GPS trackers, and other high-tech features that allow riders to track their performance, monitor their health, and stay connected with others. Smart bikes can provide valuable data to city planners and transportation officials, helping them to identify patterns of bike usage and optimize biking infrastructure. They also offer an enhanced level of safety, with features such as automatic lights and brakes that help riders avoid accidents.

3. Pedestrian-Friendly Cities

As more people embrace walking as a mode of transportation, cities around the world are beginning to prioritize pedestrian-friendly infrastructure. This includes wider sidewalks, safer crosswalks, and more green spaces to encourage walking and reduce car traffic. Pedestrian-friendly cities not only promote healthy lifestyles but also reduce the amount of pollution generated by cars, making them a more sustainable and eco-friendly option.

4. Autonomous Walking and Biking

As self-driving cars become more common, it's also possible that we will see the emergence of autonomous walking and biking. These technologies would allow pedestrians and cyclists to navigate city streets safely and efficiently, without the risk of accidents caused by distracted or negligent drivers. Autonomous bikes could also provide an eco-friendly and convenient mode of transportation for short trips within cities.

5. Hyperloop

The Hyperloop is a proposed transportation system that could revolutionize the way we travel between cities. This futuristic system would use a series of tubes and magnetic levitation to transport passengers at incredibly high speeds, potentially reaching up to 700 miles per hour. While still in the development phase, the Hyperloop has the potential to transform long-distance travel and reduce our reliance on airplanes and gas-powered cars.

Conclusion

The future of biking and pedestrian transportation is full of exciting possibilities. With the rise of e-bikes and smart bikes, as well as a growing focus on pedestrian-friendly cities, we can expect to see more people choosing these modes of transportation in the coming years. Autonomous biking and walking technologies could also provide safer, more efficient, and eco-friendly options for short trips within cities. Finally, the Hyperloop offers a glimpse into a future where long-distance travel is faster, more efficient, and more sustainable. By embracing these new technologies and prioritizing sustainable and healthy lifestyles, we can build a better future for ourselves and the planet.

Chapter 5: Drones and Flying Cars

The current state of drones and flying cars

Drones and flying cars have been a topic of discussion for many years, and recent technological advancements have made them more feasible than ever before. In this chapter, we will discuss the current state of drones and flying cars, including their current capabilities, limitations, and challenges.

Drones

Drones, also known as unmanned aerial vehicles (UAVs), have become increasingly popular in recent years. They are used in a variety of applications, including surveillance, agriculture, delivery, and entertainment. The drone market has seen significant growth in recent years, with the global market expected to reach $43 billion by 2024, according to a report by MarketsandMarkets.

Current Capabilities

Drones come in various shapes and sizes, ranging from small hobby drones to large industrial drones. They are equipped with cameras, sensors, and GPS, which allow them to fly autonomously or be controlled remotely. Drones can be used for a wide range of applications, including:

1. Surveillance: Drones are commonly used for surveillance and monitoring, particularly in areas that are

difficult to access. They can be equipped with high-resolution cameras, thermal imaging sensors, and other technologies to capture images and video footage.

2. Agriculture: Drones are used in agriculture to monitor crops, track livestock, and analyze soil and water quality. They can be equipped with sensors and cameras to collect data, which can be used to make decisions about planting, fertilizing, and harvesting crops.

3. Delivery: Drones are being developed for use in delivery, particularly in urban areas. Companies such as Amazon and UPS are exploring the use of drones for delivery of small packages.

4. Entertainment: Drones are used in entertainment, particularly in the film and television industry, to capture aerial footage and provide unique perspectives.

Limitations and Challenges

Despite their many applications, drones also have limitations and face several challenges. Some of these include:

1. Regulation: The use of drones is subject to strict regulations in many countries, particularly for commercial applications. Regulations are in place to ensure safety and prevent privacy violations.

2. Limited battery life: Drones have limited battery life, which restricts their range and flight time. This is particularly challenging for applications such as delivery, where drones need to cover long distances.

3. Weather conditions: Drones are affected by weather conditions such as wind, rain, and fog. Extreme weather conditions can make flying unsafe and restrict the use of drones.

Flying Cars

Flying cars, also known as vertical takeoff and landing (VTOL) vehicles, are another emerging technology that is capturing the public's imagination. Flying cars are being developed by companies such as Uber, Airbus, and Terrafugia.

Current Capabilities

Flying cars are still in the development phase, but several prototypes have been unveiled. These vehicles are designed to take off and land vertically, which allows them to operate in urban areas with limited space. They are being developed for use in urban transportation, with the aim of reducing traffic congestion and travel time.

Limitations and Challenges

Flying cars face several limitations and challenges that need to be addressed before they can become a viable mode of transportation. Some of these include:

1. Infrastructure: The development of flying cars requires significant infrastructure, including takeoff and landing areas and maintenance facilities. This infrastructure needs to be developed before flying cars can become a reality.

2. Cost: Flying cars are likely to be expensive, which could limit their adoption. The development of flying cars is also expensive, which could slow down their commercialization.

3. Safety: Flying cars need to be safe and reliable, particularly in urban areas where they will be operating alongside other vehicles and pedestrians. Ensuring the safety of flying.

The potential of drones and flying cars for transportation

Drones and flying cars have the potential to revolutionize the way people and goods are transported. The technology for unmanned aerial vehicles (UAVs) has been advancing rapidly over the past decade, with drones being used for a wide range of applications, from package delivery to search and rescue operations. Meanwhile, the development of electric vertical takeoff and landing (eVTOL) aircraft, also known as flying cars, has been gaining traction in recent years, with several companies working on prototypes and conducting test flights. In this section, we will explore the potential of drones and flying cars for transportation and their possible impact on society.

One of the most significant advantages of drones and flying cars is their ability to bypass traditional transportation infrastructure, such as roads and bridges. This means that they can operate in areas where traditional modes of transportation are not feasible or are slow, such as remote or congested areas. For example, drones could be used to deliver medical supplies to remote areas or to transport goods quickly and efficiently in urban areas with heavy traffic congestion. Similarly, eVTOLs could be used to transport people and goods between cities or within a city, avoiding traffic congestion and reducing travel times significantly.

Another advantage of drones and flying cars is their potential to reduce carbon emissions and improve air quality. Electric drones and eVTOLs have zero emissions during operation, making them an environmentally friendly alternative to traditional modes of transportation, such as cars and planes. This could have a significant impact on reducing air pollution in urban areas, which is a major public health issue. Additionally, the use of drones and flying cars could reduce the number of cars on the road, further reducing emissions and traffic congestion.

However, there are also several challenges that need to be addressed before drones and flying cars can become a widespread mode of transportation. One of the main challenges is safety, as accidents involving drones or eVTOLs could have serious consequences. There are also concerns around privacy and security, as drones could potentially be used for surveillance or other malicious purposes. In addition, there are regulatory and legal issues that need to be addressed, including air traffic control, pilot licensing, and liability in case of accidents.

Despite these challenges, there is significant interest and investment in the development of drones and flying cars for transportation. Several companies, including Uber and Airbus, have announced plans to develop eVTOLs for urban air mobility, and there are already commercial drone delivery services in operation in some countries. As technology advances and regulations are put in place to ensure safety and privacy, it is likely that drones and flying cars will become an increasingly important part of the transportation system in the future.

In conclusion, the potential of drones and flying cars for transportation is significant, with the ability to bypass traditional transportation infrastructure, reduce carbon emissions, and improve air quality. While there are challenges that need to be addressed, such as safety and regulatory issues, the development of these technologies is an exciting prospect for the future of transportation. As society continues to evolve, it will be interesting to see how drones and flying cars are integrated into our transportation system and the impact they have on society as a whole.

The impact of drones and flying cars on the environment

The use of drones and flying cars for transportation has the potential to revolutionize the way we move people and goods, but it also comes with environmental challenges. In this section, we will explore the impact of drones and flying cars on the environment.

1. Carbon emissions: One of the biggest environmental concerns associated with drones and flying cars is carbon emissions. The majority of these vehicles are powered by fossil fuels, which emit carbon dioxide and other greenhouse gases that contribute to climate change. While some manufacturers are exploring electric or hybrid power sources, the technology is still in its infancy and not yet widely adopted.

2. Noise pollution: Drones and flying cars also generate noise pollution, which can have negative impacts on wildlife and humans. The noise created by drones and flying cars can disrupt ecosystems and cause stress and hearing damage for people and animals in the vicinity.

3. Habitat destruction: The infrastructure needed to support drones and flying cars, such as landing pads and charging stations, can lead to habitat destruction and loss of green spaces. Additionally, if the use of these vehicles leads

to increased development and urbanization, it could have further negative impacts on the environment.

4. Air traffic congestion: As the use of drones and flying cars becomes more widespread, it could lead to air traffic congestion, which can result in increased fuel consumption and carbon emissions. Additionally, the risk of accidents and collisions could lead to environmental disasters, such as fuel spills and fires.

5. Waste and disposal: The batteries and components used in drones and flying cars can be difficult to recycle, leading to an increase in electronic waste. This could result in further environmental degradation and pollution.

Despite these environmental concerns, drones and flying cars also have the potential to be more environmentally friendly than traditional modes of transportation. For example, they could reduce the need for large, carbon-emitting vehicles for transportation, and they could reduce the need for infrastructure such as highways and parking lots.

Furthermore, the development of electric or hybrid-powered drones and flying cars could significantly reduce carbon emissions and noise pollution. Additionally, the use of renewable energy sources, such as solar or wind power, to charge and power these vehicles could further reduce their environmental impact.

In conclusion, the impact of drones and flying cars on the environment is a complex issue that requires careful consideration of the benefits and risks associated with this technology. While they have the potential to be more environmentally friendly than traditional modes of transportation, it is important to address their carbon emissions, noise pollution, habitat destruction, air traffic congestion, and waste disposal. Further research and development are needed to ensure that the potential benefits of this technology can be realized without causing undue harm to the environment.

Future developments in drones and flying cars

As drones and flying cars continue to gain popularity, there are many exciting developments and advancements happening in this field. Here are some potential future developments in drones and flying cars:

1. Increased Autonomy: One of the main challenges in the widespread use of drones and flying cars is the need for a skilled human operator to control them. However, with the advancements in artificial intelligence and machine learning, there is the potential for these vehicles to become more autonomous, eliminating the need for a human operator.

2. Better Battery Technology: Currently, the batteries used in drones and flying cars are limited in their capacity and range. However, with the development of more efficient and powerful batteries, the range of these vehicles could be greatly extended, making them more practical for longer journeys.

3. Improved Safety Features: Safety is a major concern when it comes to flying vehicles, but there are many developments happening in this area. Some potential safety features include automatic collision avoidance systems, emergency landing systems, and fail-safe mechanisms that would allow a vehicle to safely land even if one or more systems fail.

4. More Efficient Designs: Currently, many drones and flying cars are designed based on existing aircraft models. However, there is the potential for new and more efficient designs that are specifically tailored to the needs of these vehicles. This could include features such as smaller and lighter materials, more efficient propulsion systems, and more streamlined shapes.

5. Increased Integration with Existing Infrastructure: As drones and flying cars become more common, there will be a need for them to integrate with existing infrastructure such as airports and air traffic control systems. There are many developments happening in this area, including the development of new air traffic control systems specifically designed for these vehicles.

6. Urban Air Mobility: One of the most exciting potential developments in this field is the idea of urban air mobility. This would involve the use of drones and flying cars for short-haul urban transportation, such as commuting between the suburbs and the city center. There are already many companies working on developing this concept, and it has the potential to revolutionize urban transportation.

7. Air-Taxis: Another potential development in this field is the use of drones and flying cars as air-taxis. This would involve the use of these vehicles for on-demand

transportation, similar to ride-sharing services such as Uber and Lyft. There are already many companies working on developing this concept, and it has the potential to completely change the way we think about transportation.

8. Cargo Transport: In addition to passenger transportation, there is also the potential for drones and flying cars to be used for cargo transport. This could include the delivery of goods such as packages and medical supplies, and there are already many companies working on developing this concept.

9. Space Tourism: While not strictly related to drones and flying cars, the development of these vehicles has the potential to revolutionize space tourism. With the ability to travel to space becoming more accessible, there is the potential for drones and flying cars to be used for short-haul transportation within space stations and colonies.

Overall, the potential future developments in drones and flying cars are incredibly exciting, and it will be interesting to see how these vehicles continue to evolve in the coming years. With the potential for increased autonomy, better safety features, and more efficient designs, these vehicles have the potential to revolutionize transportation and completely change the way we think about getting around.

Chapter 6: Space Travel and Interplanetary Transportation

The current state of space travel and interplanetary transportation

Space travel and interplanetary transportation are two of the most exciting and challenging frontiers of modern transportation. While space travel has been a reality for several decades, the field of interplanetary transportation is still in its infancy. In this section, we will discuss the current state of space travel and interplanetary transportation.

Space Travel Space travel refers to human and robotic exploration of outer space, including activities such as launching spacecraft into orbit, rendezvous and docking, spacewalks, and exploration of other celestial bodies. The history of space travel dates back to the 1950s and 1960s when the United States and the Soviet Union began launching rockets and satellites into space. Since then, numerous countries have developed their space programs, and private companies have entered the field as well.

Currently, the International Space Station (ISS) is the only space habitat that is permanently inhabited by humans. The ISS orbits the Earth at an altitude of approximately 400 kilometers and provides a platform for scientific research, spacewalks, and technology development. Several space agencies and private companies are working on developing the technologies needed to send humans on deep-space missions, including crewed missions to Mars.

Interplanetary Transportation Interplanetary transportation refers to the transport of people and cargo between celestial bodies, such as planets, moons, and asteroids. This field is still in its early stages, and so far, only a few robotic missions have been sent to explore other celestial bodies. The most famous interplanetary mission to date is the Apollo program, which landed humans on the Moon in the late 1960s and early 1970s.

NASA and other space agencies are planning to send robotic missions to explore other planets and moons in our solar system, including Mars, Europa (a moon of Jupiter), and Titan (a moon of Saturn). These missions will provide valuable information about the geology, atmosphere, and potential habitability of these bodies.

Challenges of Space Travel and Interplanetary Transportation Space travel and interplanetary transportation face several challenges, including technological, financial, and safety issues. The following are some of the major challenges:

1. Propulsion: The current technologies for space travel and interplanetary transportation rely on chemical

rockets, which have limited capabilities for deep-space missions. Developing more efficient and powerful propulsion systems is essential for sending humans and cargo on deep-space missions.

2. Radiation: Deep-space missions expose humans and spacecraft to high levels of radiation, which can damage equipment and cause health problems for astronauts. Developing effective shielding and protection against radiation is critical for long-duration missions.

3. Life support: Long-duration space missions require the development of sustainable life support systems, including food, water, and air recycling, to support human survival.

4. Cost: Space travel and interplanetary transportation are extremely expensive, with a high cost per kilogram of payload. Finding ways to reduce the cost of space exploration and transportation is essential for the development of these fields.

5. Safety: Space travel and interplanetary transportation are inherently risky, and accidents can have catastrophic consequences. Ensuring the safety of astronauts and equipment is a top priority for space agencies and private companies.

Conclusion

In conclusion, space travel and interplanetary transportation are exciting and challenging fields that have the potential to revolutionize our understanding of the universe and our place in it. Despite the challenges, significant progress has been made in these fields, and we can expect to see continued advances in the coming years.

The potential of space travel and interplanetary transportation for future transportation needs

Space travel and interplanetary transportation have long been a subject of fascination and intrigue for humanity. While space travel is still in its infancy, there is a growing potential for its use in future transportation needs.

One of the main potential uses for space travel and interplanetary transportation is for long-distance travel between different points on Earth. While current modes of transportation, such as planes, can cover long distances quickly, space travel could provide a faster and more efficient alternative. For example, a trip from New York to Tokyo currently takes around 14 hours by plane, but with space travel, this journey could potentially be completed in just a few hours. This could greatly benefit business and international trade, as well as personal travel.

Another potential use for space travel and interplanetary transportation is for space tourism. With the rise of private space companies such as SpaceX and Blue Origin, space tourism is becoming a reality. The potential for space tourism could have a significant impact on the transportation industry, as it could open up a whole new market for travel and leisure.

Furthermore, space travel and interplanetary transportation have the potential to revolutionize transportation in areas where traditional modes of transportation are difficult or impossible. For example, in remote and rural areas, where transportation infrastructure is often lacking or non-existent, space travel could provide a fast and efficient way to transport goods and people.

Interplanetary transportation could also provide a solution to resource depletion on Earth. As resources become scarce on our planet, space exploration could provide a means of extracting resources from other planets and asteroids. This could help to sustain our civilization for generations to come.

In addition to the potential uses for space travel and interplanetary transportation, there are also numerous technological advancements that are being made in this field. For example, advancements in rocket technology and space vehicle design are making space travel more accessible and safer. Additionally, the development of reusable rockets and space vehicles is helping to reduce the cost of space travel, making it more feasible for commercial use.

Overall, while space travel and interplanetary transportation are still in the early stages of development, they have a significant potential for use in future transportation needs. From long-distance travel to space tourism and resource extraction, the possibilities are endless. As technology continues to advance and space travel becomes more accessible, it will be exciting to see how this field develops and impacts the future of transportation.

The impact of space travel and interplanetary transportation on the environment

Space travel and interplanetary transportation are still in their infancy, and their environmental impact is not yet fully understood. However, as technology advances and humans explore deeper into space, it is important to consider the potential environmental impacts of these activities.

The Impact of Rocket Launches One of the most immediate and visible impacts of space travel is the environmental impact of rocket launches. Rockets emit large amounts of greenhouse gases, including carbon dioxide and nitrogen oxides, which contribute to global climate change. Additionally, rockets produce large amounts of noise pollution, which can have negative impacts on local wildlife and ecosystems.

The Impact of Space Debris Space debris, or man-made objects orbiting the Earth, is another environmental concern associated with space travel. These objects can pose a threat to satellites, spacecraft, and even humans, and they can also contribute to the buildup of space debris, which can have negative impacts on Earth's environment. For example, if a satellite or other space debris falls to Earth, it can release hazardous materials into the atmosphere.

The Impact of Space Mining As humans begin to explore and potentially exploit resources on other planets and asteroids, space mining may become a reality. This could have significant environmental impacts, as mining activities can contribute to deforestation, erosion, and water pollution. Additionally, the extraction and processing of resources in space could produce greenhouse gas emissions and other forms of pollution.

Mitigating the Environmental Impacts of Space Travel To mitigate the environmental impacts of space travel, it is important to continue developing and implementing sustainable technologies and practices. For example, rocket manufacturers can develop more efficient propulsion systems and use renewable energy sources to power their facilities. Additionally, space agencies can work to reduce the amount of space debris through active debris removal initiatives and responsible satellite and spacecraft design.

Conclusion While space travel and interplanetary transportation offer exciting possibilities for the future of transportation, it is important to consider their potential environmental impacts. By continuing to develop sustainable technologies and practices, we can minimize these impacts and ensure a healthy and sustainable future for our planet.

Future developments in space travel and interplanetary transportation

Space travel and interplanetary transportation have come a long way since the first human spaceflight in 1961. The future of space exploration and travel is promising, with many new technologies and advancements being developed to make space travel safer, more efficient, and more affordable. In this section, we will explore some of the most exciting future developments in space travel and interplanetary transportation.

1. Space Tourism

Space tourism is an emerging market that is expected to grow in the coming years. Companies such as SpaceX, Blue Origin, and Virgin Galactic are working on developing spacecraft that can carry tourists to space. These spacecraft will be equipped with state-of-the-art technology and will provide a unique experience to their passengers.

In the future, space tourism is expected to become more affordable, and many more people will be able to experience space travel. With advancements in technology, spacecraft will become safer and more reliable, and travel times to space will be reduced.

2. Interplanetary Transportation

Mars has been a focus of many space agencies and private companies for years. NASA is planning to send humans to Mars in the 2030s, and SpaceX has announced plans to send humans to Mars as early as 2024. The development of the Starship spacecraft by SpaceX is a major step towards achieving this goal.

In the future, we can expect more missions to Mars and other planets, including the Moon. These missions will be aimed at establishing a permanent human presence on other planets and conducting scientific research.

3. Space Mining

Space mining is the process of extracting minerals and other resources from asteroids and other celestial bodies. With advancements in technology, space mining is becoming more feasible, and many companies are investing in this emerging market.

In the future, space mining could provide a sustainable source of resources for human exploration and habitation in space. It could also have a significant impact on the global economy by providing access to rare minerals and other resources.

4. Space-Based Solar Power

Space-based solar power is the concept of collecting solar energy in space and transmitting it to Earth. This could provide a sustainable source of energy for the planet, as well as help reduce greenhouse gas emissions.

In the future, space-based solar power could become a major source of renewable energy for the planet. It could also have a significant impact on the global economy by providing a new market for space technology and services.

5. Advanced Propulsion Systems

Propulsion systems are a critical component of space travel and interplanetary transportation. Advances in propulsion technology could significantly reduce travel times and make space travel more efficient and cost-effective.

In the future, we can expect to see the development of advanced propulsion systems such as nuclear propulsion and ion thrusters. These systems could significantly reduce travel times to other planets and make interstellar travel more feasible.

Conclusion

The future of space travel and interplanetary transportation is exciting and promising. With advancements in technology and the development of new spacecraft and propulsion systems, we can expect to see significant progress in the coming years. Space tourism, interplanetary transportation, space mining, space-based solar power, and advanced propulsion systems are just a few of the many areas of development in space exploration. These developments have the potential to transform the way we live and work, and usher in a new era of human exploration and discovery.

Conclusion

The importance of developing alternative modes of transportation

As the world's population continues to grow, transportation has become an increasingly important aspect of modern life. However, our current reliance on fossil fuels to power our transportation systems has created significant environmental challenges. From air pollution to climate change, the negative impacts of transportation on the environment are undeniable. In order to mitigate these impacts and ensure a sustainable future, it is essential that we develop alternative modes of transportation that are both environmentally friendly and efficient.

The importance of developing alternative modes of transportation cannot be overstated. Not only will it help reduce the negative impacts of transportation on the environment, but it will also provide a host of other benefits. For example, alternative modes of transportation can help reduce traffic congestion, improve public health, and increase access to transportation in underserved communities. Additionally, alternative modes of transportation can help reduce our dependence on foreign oil, thereby increasing national security.

One of the most promising alternative modes of transportation is electric vehicles (EVs). EVs have already gained significant traction in the automotive industry, with many major manufacturers now offering electric models. EVs offer several advantages over traditional gasoline-powered vehicles, including reduced emissions and lower operating costs. As battery technology continues to improve, the range and performance of EVs will only continue to increase, making them an increasingly viable option for transportation.

Another promising alternative mode of transportation is public transit. Buses, trains, and other forms of public transit offer several advantages over private vehicles, including reduced congestion and emissions. Public transit also provides an affordable and accessible option for transportation, especially for those who may not have access to a private vehicle. As technology continues to improve, public transit systems will become even more efficient and accessible, further reducing their environmental impact.

Bikes and pedestrian transportation are also important alternative modes of transportation. Biking and walking offer several benefits, including improved health and reduced emissions. In urban areas, biking and walking can be a practical alternative to driving, especially for short trips.

As cities continue to invest in bike lanes and pedestrian infrastructure, biking and walking will become even more accessible and safe.

In addition to these alternative modes of transportation, emerging technologies such as drones and flying cars have the potential to revolutionize transportation in the future. While still in their early stages of development, these technologies offer the promise of faster and more efficient transportation, while also reducing congestion and emissions. However, it is important to carefully consider the potential environmental impacts of these technologies as they continue to develop.

Overall, developing alternative modes of transportation is essential for a sustainable future. By reducing our reliance on fossil fuels and prioritizing environmentally friendly transportation options, we can create a cleaner, healthier, and more efficient transportation system. However, it will require significant investment and innovation from both the public and private sectors to make this a reality. It is our responsibility to prioritize sustainable transportation solutions and work towards a better future for ourselves and future generations.

The potential of new technologies for transportation

The world of transportation is rapidly changing, and new technologies are emerging every day. From electric cars to hyperloops, the potential for new transportation technologies to revolutionize the way we move around is vast. In this section, we will explore some of the most promising new technologies for transportation and their potential impact on the future of mobility.

One of the most exciting new technologies for transportation is autonomous vehicles. These vehicles, which are capable of driving themselves without human intervention, have the potential to reduce traffic congestion, improve safety, and increase accessibility for those who are unable to drive. Autonomous vehicles are already being tested on public roads in some parts of the world, and companies like Google and Tesla are investing heavily in the development of this technology.

Another promising new technology for transportation is the hyperloop. This is a high-speed transportation system that involves pods traveling through vacuum-sealed tubes at speeds of up to 700 miles per hour. The hyperloop has the potential to drastically reduce travel times between cities and could revolutionize long-distance travel. Companies like Virgin Hyperloop are currently testing this technology, and it is possible that we could see hyperloops become a viable transportation option in the near future.

In addition to autonomous vehicles and hyperloops, there are many other new technologies that are being developed for transportation. Electric planes, for example, have the potential to significantly reduce carbon emissions from air travel, while flying taxis could provide a faster and more efficient way to get around congested cities. In the realm of space travel, companies like SpaceX are developing reusable rockets that could make space travel more affordable and accessible.

Despite the potential benefits of these new technologies, there are also concerns about their impact on society and the environment. Autonomous vehicles, for example, could lead to job losses for those who work in the transportation industry, while the hyperloop could have a significant impact on the communities it passes through. In addition, the materials and energy required to produce and operate these new technologies could have a significant environmental impact.

As we move forward with the development of new transportation technologies, it is important that we carefully consider their potential impact and take steps to mitigate any negative effects. This could involve developing new regulations to ensure the safe and equitable deployment of these technologies, investing in sustainable materials and energy sources, and working with communities to address any concerns they may have about new transportation infrastructure.

In conclusion, new technologies have the potential to revolutionize the way we move around and address many of the challenges facing our current transportation systems. However, it is important that we approach these technologies with caution and carefully consider their potential impact on society and the environment. By doing so, we can ensure that we are creating a transportation system that is safe, efficient, and sustainable for all.

The need for collaboration between industries and governments for a sustainable future

As we've explored in this book, alternative modes of transportation and new technologies have the potential to revolutionize the way we move around in the world. However, the adoption of these new technologies and transportation modes requires collaboration between industries and governments to ensure that we create a sustainable future.

The transportation sector is responsible for a significant portion of global greenhouse gas emissions, which contribute to climate change. To reduce these emissions, we need to focus on developing and adopting alternative modes of transportation and new technologies that are more environmentally friendly. But this cannot be achieved by a single industry or government alone; it requires collaboration between different industries and governments at both the national and international levels.

One of the most significant challenges facing the transportation sector is the lack of infrastructure and policies to support alternative modes of transportation. For example, the infrastructure for electric vehicles is still lacking in many countries, and the charging network is not yet as widespread as it needs to be. Governments need to work with industry players to invest in and develop this infrastructure, create policies that encourage the adoption of alternative modes of transportation, and incentivize the development of environmentally friendly technologies.

Another critical area of collaboration is in the development of regulations and standards. As new technologies and transportation modes emerge, it's crucial to establish regulations and standards that ensure safety and sustainability. Governments and industry players must work together to create these regulations and standards to prevent safety risks and ensure that we are moving towards a more sustainable future.

Furthermore, collaboration is essential in the research and development of new technologies. Governments and industry players need to invest in research and development to create new, innovative technologies that can revolutionize the way we move around. Collaboration between different industries can bring together different perspectives and expertise, leading to the development of new technologies that are more efficient and sustainable.

Finally, collaboration between governments and industry players is crucial in educating the public on the importance of sustainable transportation. Governments can create policies and incentives to encourage the adoption of alternative modes of transportation, but the public needs to be aware of these options and their benefits. Industry players can also play a role in educating the public on the new technologies and transportation modes available to them.

In conclusion, the transportation sector has the potential to create a sustainable future by adopting alternative modes of transportation and new technologies. However, achieving this requires collaboration between different industries and governments. By working together to invest in infrastructure, establish regulations and standards, and develop new technologies, we can create a transportation system that is more efficient, sustainable, and environmentally friendly.

THE END

Key Terms and Definitions

To help you better understand the language and concepts related to aging and older adults, below you will find a list of key terms and their definitions.

Key terms and definitions:

1. Transportation: The movement of people, goods, or services from one place to another.

2. Sustainability: The ability to meet the needs of the present without compromising the ability of future generations to meet their own needs.

3. Alternative fuels: Any fuel other than gasoline or diesel that can be used to power vehicles, such as electricity, hydrogen, biofuels, and natural gas.

4. Autonomous vehicles: Self-driving vehicles that use sensors and software to navigate and control the vehicle.

5. Biodiesel: A renewable fuel made from vegetable oil, animal fat, or recycled restaurant grease.

6. Electric vehicles (EVs): Vehicles that run on electricity stored in batteries or fuel cells.

7. Interplanetary transportation: Transportation between planets or celestial bodies in space.

8. Public transit: Any mode of transportation that is available to the public, such as buses, trains, and light rail.

9. Smart transportation: The use of technology to improve the efficiency, safety, and sustainability of transportation systems.

10. Sustainable transportation: Transportation systems and modes that are environmentally friendly, socially equitable, and economically viable.

11. Urban mobility: The movement of people and goods within urban areas, including public transportation, biking, walking, and micro-mobility options such as scooters and e-bikes.

12. Zero-emission vehicles: Vehicles that emit no tailpipe emissions, such as battery electric vehicles, hydrogen fuel cell vehicles, and plug-in hybrid electric vehicles.

Supporting Materials

Introduction:

- International Energy Agency. (2019). Global EV Outlook 2019: Scaling-up the transition to electric mobility. Paris, France.

Chapter 1: Ships and Boats:

- IMO. (2021). Energy Efficiency Measures for Ships. International Maritime Organization.

Chapter 2: Trains and Railways:

- International Union of Railways. (2021). High-Speed Rail 2021: A Review of Fast Passenger Services Worldwide. Brussels, Belgium.

Chapter 3: Buses and Public Transit:

- American Public Transportation Association. (2019). Public Transportation Fact Book. Washington, D.C.

- International Association of Public Transport. (2021). Public transport trends report 2021. Brussels, Belgium.

Chapter 4: Bikes and Pedestrian Transportation:

- National Academies of Sciences, Engineering, and Medicine. (2018). The safety and health of pedestrians, bicyclists, and motorcyclists. Washington, D.C.

- Pucher, J., & Buehler, R. (2012). City cycling. Cambridge, MA: MIT Press.

Chapter 5: Drones and Flying Cars:

- Dufour, P. (2020). Electric VTOL Aircraft and Urban Air Mobility: A Clean Future for Aviation? Oxford, UK: Elsevier.
- Hesselink, H., & Mooij, E. (2018). Electric Urban Air Mobility: Unpacking the Opportunities, Challenges and Risks. Hague, Netherlands: Netherlands Aerospace Centre.

Chapter 6: Space Travel and Interplanetary Transportation:
- National Aeronautics and Space Administration. (2020). NASA's Planetary Science Vision 2050. Washington, D.C.
- International Academy of Astronautics. (2020). The Space Transportation Roadmap: Recommendations on Opportunities and Challenges. Paris, France.

Conclusion:
- United Nations. (2015). Paris Agreement - Status of Ratification. New York, NY: United Nations.
- International Energy Agency. (2020). World Energy Outlook 2020. Paris, France.

www.ingramcontent.com/pod-product-compliance
Lightning Source LLC
LaVergne TN
LVHW021052100526
838202LV00083B/5830